The World Historian as Poet

The World Historian as *Poet*

David Kopf

12/28/06
To Clara,
in appreciation
for the
wonderful
things all did
with Bob
and Di
over the
years
Best Wishes,
David

North Star Press of St. Cloud, Inc.
St. Cloud, Minnesota

Cover art by: Walter Kopf

ISBN: 0-87839-243-2

Printed in the United States of America

Published by
North Star Press of St. Cloud, Inc.
P.O. Box 451
St. Cloud, Minnesota 56302
northstarpress.com

Acknowledgements

I should like to thank Professor Emerita Jane Betts for her willingness to write the foreword for this volume. Jane is a highly creative and imaginative poet who has been a source of inspiration for me. I should also wish to express my appreciation to Jane's husband, Donald Betts, a highly gifted performer, composer, and professor of classical piano music, for his warm friendship and sage advice in matters of art and intellect over the years. His encouragement of my poetic endeavors will not be forgotten.

My thanks to my son Walter, who has mastered the intricacies of painting these several years and has recently turned his attention to the art of etching. Besides providing the illustrations for this book, he has offered constructive criticism, which I believe has greatly improved the ideational quality of the poetry.

I am grateful to Dr. Ghulam Murshid, whose masterful biography of Michael Mudhusudan Dutt, the most outstanding poet of the Indian Renaissance in Bengal, was an incredibly rich learning experience for me in ascertaining the subtleties of writing poetry in cross-cultural perspective.

It is to Mary Pat Johnson, celebrated teacher and inveterate world traveler, that I owe a great debt of gratitude for critiquing my poems and convincing me that many of them had sufficient literary merit to be worthy of publication. Pat's experience with a prominent Minneapolis book club has been very beneficial in the preparation of this book.

About the Author

David Kopf received his Ph.D. in the history of India at the University of Chicago and is currently professor emeritus in the Department of History at the University of Minnesota. Kopf's historical monographs include: *British Orientalism and the Bengal Renaissance* (Berkeley, 1969), which won the Watumull Prize awarded by the American Historical Association in 1969 and *The Brahmo Samaj and the Shaping of the Modern Indian Mind* (Princeton, 1979). In the 1980s Kopf's interests widened as he introduced World History as an undergraduate course in his department. As a result of seminars with his colleagues in Asian History, they brought out a two-volume work, *The Comparative History of Civilization in Asia* (Westview Press, 1986). Kopf was among the earliest contributing editors of the World History Association's official Journal of World History and served as vice-president of the International Society for the Comparative Study of Civilization.

In the 1990s, Kopf carried on scholarly research in total war and genocide in the twentieth century. He collaborated with eric Markusen in the publication of *The Holocaust and Strategic Bombing* (Westview Press, 1995), which was strongly endorsed by Daniel Ellsberg and Robert J. Lifton, among others. In the same year, Kopf brought out a novel, *Scratches on Kali's Mind*, which deal with the politics of nationalism, war, and revolution in South Asia during the period of the 1971 Indo-Pakistan war, which led to the birth of Bangladesh.

Kopf has been awarded grants by the Ford Foundation, Fulbright, the American Institute of Indian Studies, and Guggenheim, to carry on research on different facets of modern South Asian history. In addition, he has published fifty articles and has lectured widely around the world.

In the present volume, Kopf seeks to add poetry to scholarship and creative fiction as a valid dimension in our deepening study of world history. Hopefully, this book should demonstrate that poetry may well transcend the often rigid confines of objective methodology and historiography, thus liberating and enlightening our perspective about crucial ideas on the meaning of historical events. The qualities of the poetic dimension may also supplement attempts to understand history by means of fictional prose.

Kopf has organized the poetry chronologically within four sections: "A Catalogue of Impressionable Experiences," "Cultural Insights and Images," "World History and the Philosophy of Life," and "The Romantic Lover and His Conversion to the Church of Eros." In the first section, Kopf endeavors to transform impressionable narratives of the world around him into more compact expressions of the basic ideas intended. The poems in section two are mainly about world travel, but unlike those in the first section, these reflect a deeper personal and intellectual experience associated with a given place. In the third section, Kopf shifts from his poetic focus on world travel to history and philosophy unencumbered by the customary mountains of scholarly prose. The final section represents a period in Kopf's career when he was greatly influenced by the traditions of erotic mysticism in the religions of the world. In this section, also, Kopf explores his own feelings and attitudes.

Contents

Acknowledgements v
Foreword 1

Catalogue of Impressionable Experiences

Mendelssohn Alongside Hollywood Beach, Florida, 1948 **9**
Reunion with My Mother, 1948 **11**
The Importance of Being "Ernest," 1949 **13**
Havanna, 1949 B.C. (Before Castro) **15**
First Hangover, 1950 **17**
Early Morn at Summer Camp, 1950 **18**
A Summer View from the Summit of Garret Mountain, 1950 **19**
Autumn Scene, 1950 **20**
From Our Apartment Window on Ho Chi Minh Serani, 1961 **21**
Return to Calcutta, 1962 **23**
Dedicated to My Friend Who Pocketed Ashtrays, 1973 **25**
My Friend's Cabin, 1975 **27**
Sewer City Is in Everyland, 1976 **29**
Episode on the Bangladeshi Riviera, 1976 **31**
A Snail's Pace in a Snail's World on a Sandy Beach, 1978 **33**
On Turning Fifty, 1980 **35**
Images from Hiking on Signal Mountain on the Irish West Coast, 1994 **36**
Prague Impressions, 2003 **38**
Impressions of Cinque Terre, 2003 **40**

Cultural Insights and Images

Maya Leads Me by the Nose, 1987 **43**
The Tourist Who Captured a Soul, 1962 **45**
Globalization in Southeast Asia, 1962 (1903) **47**
The Great Banares Circus, 1962 **49**
The Pink City of Jaipur, 1983 **52**
Kibbutz, 1963 **54**
Iran, 1963 **56**
April in Paris, 1963 **59**
Ah, to Be in England in the Spring of 1963 **61**
Twelve Views of Bharat (India), 1964 **63**
Caricature and National Identity in the 1960s: India and Israel, 1964 **65**
War and Genocide Across the Border in Bangladesh, 1971 **68**
The Man Who Chased Sunsets with His Camera, 1971 **69**
Taj Mahal: Visit to a Martyr's Tomb, 1980 **71**
Casablanca, 1994 **72**
Icelandic Images, 1997 **73**
Milan in the Age of Globalization, 2003 **75**
Thoughts of Death and Dying on a Rhone River Cruise, 2003 **76**
Mazatlan, 2003 **77**
The Educational Impact of Auschwitz, 2004 **78**

World History and the Philosophy of Life

Henry Derozio; Influential Hindu College Teacher, 1962 **83**
William Carey, Father of Modern Bengali Prose, 1964 **85**
Sir William Jones and the Positive Side of British Colonialism, 1967 **87**
Orientalism, 1969 **89**
Angkor and Humanity's Fate Written on the Sands of Penang, 1971 **91**

Rammohun Roy: Father of Modern India, 1973 **93**
Durga Puja (Homage to the Goddess Durga), 1979 **95**
Hinduism, 1979 **97**
The Whole World Is a Jew, 1979 **99**
A Father's Advice to the Newlyweds, 1989 **100**
A Day of Meditation and Peace at the Lake, 1983 **101**
The Three Faces of Truth (December 31, 1999) **102**
An Obscure Obituary Notice: Our Century as a Burial Ground, 1999 **104**
Sharing with Walter the Wisdom of the Upanishads, 2002 **106**
Reaction to Those Dying Around Me, 2005 **107**
Looking Ahead to an Afternoon in the Global Year, 2050 A.D. **109**

The Romantic Lover and His Conversion to the Church of Eros

Isolation and the Pangs of Remorse, 1948 **113**
First Poem of Loving Encounters with Susan, 1948 **114**
Confessions of an Eighteen-Year-Old Romantic, 1948 **115**
Memories of Love and Marriage, 1974 **116**
From Bangladesh to Bennington (Paradise Regained), 1975 **120**
The Church of Eros, 1975 **122**
A Promenade with My Love in a Bangladeshi Jungle, 1975 **123**
Muslim Woman, 1975 **125**
Reverence for the Divine Woman as a Multi-Faceted Goddess, 1979 **127**
Transformation, 1985 **129**
My Love and the Loveless Object of My Love, 2000 **131**
To My New Friend, 2000 **133**
Love and Virginity, 2001 **134**
Attributes of My Beloved, 2003 **135**
My Chinese Woman of the World, 2004 **136**
Ode to the Blue and White Football Jersey, 2004 **139**

Foreword

Poetry from the World

David Kopf has entitled this volume of collected poems written over a lifetime of study and travel *The World Historian as Poet.* "World historian" is a term and a role that has come into the academic parlance as of the last quarter of the twentieth century. The professor of World History is no longer a Middle Eastern scholar or an Asian Studies person, but a teacher who treats all areas as a part of the whole earth, the problems and fortunes of one area intersecting or even imitating those of another.

This expansiveness in geographical history in Professor Kopf's case is enhanced by the breadth of years in which he has observed the movements of history and culture. From the age of thirteen to the present age of seventy-five, he has kept meticulous journals every day—journals that show an acute sensitivity to the outer world and its effect on his own life. It is from these journals that the poetry arose, and here they are—starting in 1948 with his first trip away from home to college and ending with nostalgia over a football jersey previously borrowed by a woman who has since left him. In between these two personal poems are the views of a world traveler, for David Kopf has traveled to or has lived in India, Bangladesh, Indonesia, Israel, Iran, just about every country in Europe, as well as Iceland, Mexico, and Northern Africa. He has published two important books on modern Indian history, one of which earned the Watamull Prize, given to him by the American Historical Society for the best study on India for 1969. His immersion in Indian culture is apparent in his novel *Scratches on the Mind of Kali,* in which Americans are changed by their meeting with Indian culture and Indians are impressed by Western modernism.

Unlike the usual new Post-Colonialist candidate being hired by academic departments today, Kopf, after a lifetime of study, is not afraid to be what is considered politically incorrect in several ways. He gives credit to colonialists for what has been contributed to the regaining of the colony's culture or history. He uses Orientalism as a proud term, and he has the *chutspa* to use the word "Jew" as a derogatory term.

Only a Jew could get away with that last one and David Kopf is what could be called a secular Jew, brought up in the New Jersey town of Paterson by the kind of Orthodox Jewish mother who, later on a trip, would bring her grown son a cooked chicken in her suitcase. Kopf shows both the suffering and the pride in being Jewish. Two of his strongest poems appropriate the negative connotations of denigration or horrors of the label to other intolerances and the often resulting atrocious events. In a satirical way, he employs the term "Jew" as everybody's derogatory word for the despised other. The imagery is striking, even shocking, at once playful and terrible.

Does not the American black
wear his skin
like the nose of a Jew?

"Look carefully / at your neighbor / or yourself," he warns, "and you will find a Jew."

In "The Educational Impact of Auschwitz 2004," Kopf gives a shocking twist to the Holocaust by combining academic terminology with the atrocities as in the phrases "Mass Murder 101" or "the Hallowed Halls of Auschwitz" to convey the intellectual's indifference to the horrors, and he broadens out the lessons learned from Auschwitz to other historical or contemporary genocides. Genocide is a theme of prime importance to Professor Kopf as it is to poet Kopf. In his book, written in collaboration with sociology professor Eric Markusen, entitled *The Holocaust and Strategic Bombing: Genocide and Total War in the Twentieth Century*, he makes the case that genocide and war visited on civilians in an effort to wipe out huge cities are really the same thing: mass murder.

Kopf says this of his own relationship to the culture that raised him:

I have endured
my share
of self reproach
after years of alienation
from the Judeo-Christian ethic.

His pride in Judaism is apparent, however, in his glowing praise of the Kibbutz in the poem written in 1963. He points out that these refugees from the Diaspora raise "great crops / all cultivated / by city Jews / who have never smelled manure."

The years of living and visiting in India have left their mark on Kopf's attitude toward history, religion, and women. As I have said, he is not at all reluctant to point to Western accomplishments in India. He praises those persons who have brought about a Renaissance in Indian culture, resurrected Sanskrit from antiquity, and helped shape Bengali prose, and he speaks of the positive side of British Colonialism. He uses the term Orientalism positively even though he is well aware of its disuse by the politically correct and knows from experience the falsity of the Indian caricature. He shows great respect for Hinduism in a number of these poems, and he loves the Upanishads with their feeling of the light within and their opposition to diversity of race and class. His poem of advice to his son and another on instructions upon his son's marriage are scaffolded on the Upanishads and Hinduism. But, alas, the ancient culture so recently unearthed for modern times is being reburied by globalization:

Which God
does India worship today
The Avatar Krishna
or computer science?

This clinging to traditional cultures is an effort on Kopf's part to find calm in the presence of the growing number of threatening incursions by globalization against those cultures. To treat the globe as one in a philosophical sense does not mean he ceases to find disturbing the culture of a great ancient society going down the tubes in the face of popularization. In the poem "Hinduism," Kopf writes, "I have been told / that God is the drink of India," but the poem ends with describing the Hindus this way:

people at the mercy
of a congenital epidemic
of weariness.

Just as he had predicted so well, the results of globalization in "Southeast Asia in 1962," Kopf sees the choice for Middle Eastern Iran between Islam and her Persian heritage as far back as 1963. He hopes for a renaissance after becoming acquainted with the aristocratic Iranians, including the Shah, and being inspired by the remains of the ancient Golden City of Persepolis. We all know only too well now how that decision turned out. The poems in this book are divided into three sections and each might appeal to a certain audience, though certainly not limited to its members. The first, called "A Catalogue of Impressional Experiences," will appeal to those who like nature hikes, adventure in foreign places, mountain views, and a youthful lyricism that reflects the author's moods rather than specifically describing the country's culture or distinctions.

The second section, called "World History and the Philosophy of Life," is for the intellectual who wants his interest in travel to be a means of education and is interested in historical and political attitudes and in getting an honest but colorful view of the country being written about.

The third section, called "The Romantic Lover and the Church of Eros," will claim the attention of women and mainstream feminists, in particular. It goes beyond showing appreciation of the women he has known in one way or another from a variety of backgrounds in his life. (David is a lover of women and seems to remain friendly with them even after the passion has cooled.) It argues for an appreciation of the feminine side in a larger psychological sense based on the Hindu female god construct.

Sakti is the Hindu god
as woman
worshiped in her many aspects:
Lakshmi is wealth, Saraswati is music and art
Kami is love, Kali is death
and Durga is the goddess as mother.

This poem, found in the middle section explaining the goddess, is elaborated on in the Eros section under the telling title "Reverence for the Divine Woman as a Multi-Faceted Goddess, 1979." In his poem of advice to his children, in his feeling of understanding of the liberalism of a Catholic woman friend, in his empathy for the suffering of Moslem women, like that of the wife he calls "virginally enshrined" in the Taj Mahal after fourteen childbirths—all show real empathy for women. Kopf describes what he calls his conversion to the church of Eros, but it is actually more of a realization of the way in which the feminine god of Hinduism in her diversity of aspects has liberated him to partake of a diversity of relationships with women and to discover the power of the feminine side. There is a strange cross-cultural thing going on here between the Greco-Roman Eros and the Hindu Kami (et al).

Women may look at Kopf's poem about his marriage years a little ambiguously, however, especially if they are or have been academic wives, for he puts all the events of the marriage, particularly the births of his children, in terms of affording them when he has moved ahead from one academic stage to another, in other words, in terms of being the male provider. This male stance can be viewed as touching but also as a little self-centered by women in general, remembering the throes of labor pangs.

These three divisions are each chronologically arranged from early poems to the most current, and the poetics are the same in all three sections. The poems are written in the short-lined free verse of the Imagists that Kopf probably first heard in the Ninety-second Street YMHA in the famous series of poets reading their own works, including William Carlos Williams. Some of the lines in this poetry are very relaxed, some use allusions humorously like these lines:

> Ah to be in England
> Now that spring is here
> Ach, to be in England
> Who needs it?

Or ironically,

> But in the jungle
> of human encirclement
> do unto others
> before they do unto you.

Some of Kopf's lines reach the status of high poetry as in the conclusion of the philosophical poem "The Three Faces of Truth (December 31, 1999)." This ultimate existential question forms part of the third kind of truth, the nitty-gritty kind, not that of science or common sense, but of a deep sense of human confrontation with the real natural order of things:

> Why are we born
> when we live all too briefly
> and die forever?

Jane Colville Betts, Professor Emerita
University of Wisconsin, Eau Claire

Catalogue of Impressionable Experiences

ཀ༄

Mendelssohn Alongside Hollywood Beach, Florida, 1948

This is perhaps my first attempt while a student at the University of Miami of transforming a long-winded impressionable narrative into a more compact, precise expression of the idea intended. This succinct expression of an idea is how I came to define the poetry I was writing.

As Hollywood Beach town
drew near,
the brightness
of Miami Beach
vanished in the noonday sun.
The encroaching darkness
carpeted the sea
just as Mendelssohn's Fifth Symphony
was richly orchestrated
in the small space
of the car.
Outside,
one hundred yards distant,
lay the menacing ocean;
but within,
I became helplessly entranced
by a disarming
and soothing melody.
The harsh beauty
of the ocean's wild fury
was soon juxtaposed
with Mendelssohn's peasant village;
and in my mind's eye,
colorfully-clad
young men and women
danced their hearts away.
Suddenly,
a curve in the road
and the choppy sea
loomed ever closer.
The symphonic sounds

are silent now.
The car is parked
and only the birds are in view
above the oceanic expanse.
Then they grow
ever smaller
as they fly
into the encroaching,
light-failing sky
and are seen no more.

Reunion with My Mother, 1948

Here is a second example of an impressionable narrative being transformed into a more succinct expression of the main thought. On this occasion, my mother came to visit me during Christmas break at the University of Miami. It should be kept in mind that the original narrative was over four pages long.

One of the persons
who stepped off the plane
in Miami
gave birth to me;
and herself,
had been born in a Polish town,
which I looked for once
but could never find.
Mother and son,
intensely affectionate
following
three months of separation.
In Miami Beach,
we sat in the hot sun
sharing the joy
of her loving heart.
I took
the moist-eyed lady's hand
in mine
and raised it
to my lips.
Only when we devoured a knish
between us,
did I picture my dad
entering the house
on a cold, bleak night.
I wished
to reach out to him
but the distance
that separated us
could not be measured
in mileage.

My mom and I
walked to the beach
and looked straight
at the dark sea.
A new chapter opened
on seaside retreats
in the book of her soul.

The Importance of Being "Ernest," 1949

In this poem, the sensitive adolescent who found himself studying ornithology among other courses, identifies with the writer, Ernest Hemingway. By some sense of ego gratification, observing birds became an activity associated with hunting and fishing.

Hemingway and I share
a slow ride down Dixie Highway
between tomato plants, bird farms, and snake labs.
Then to quench papa's thirst,
we each down three beers
at Simmons Barin Homestead,
half-way between Miami and Key West.

Ernest first fished
where large hawks and cranes circled
in the windless sky above a low reef.
Then he waited for a bite
on viaduct number five,
swinging his rod overhead
hopefully casting for a prize.
In the end, he was consoled
with the catch of a small grunt,
the not-so-distant cousin of a snapper.
The mighty Hemingway
endured fruitless fishing once more
near the Bodiah Honda Bridge.

Somewhere, at his request,
we picked up a drunken sailor
AWOL from the Boca Chica Naval Base.
Then the night flew by
from darkness to dawn,
as we guzzled beer in a pub
on Truman Ave in Key West.

Hemingway welcomed the sunrise
at Sugar Loaf Key
with a steady rhythmic snore;
I, in turn, greeted that splash of colors
across the heavenly canvas
with a monstrous aching head.

Then I am back in Miami, at sunset,
my self-image free of Ernest;
I am I once more,
in the arms of Susan, my darling.

Havana, 1949 B.C. (Before Castro)

Here, it is not simply an impressional narrative I am transforming into a poem, but an unfinished novel on Havana. The title, Sing We for Love and Idleness, *is taken from an early lyrical poem by Ezra Pound.*

My first adventure
beyond American shores
was for rest and recreation in Cuba.
I was told
at the University of Miami,
that Havana was the site
of Satan's pleasure dome,
offering a never-ending feast
for the mind, body, and spirit.

At the cafés
encircling Havana University,
students exchanged gossipy intelligence
in flawless *gringo* English.
I listened with an anthropologist's ear
for native cultural insights,
but all I recall were the stereotypes of
Yankeeland
floating easily
on the canals of our conversation.

How lovely in my mind's eye
were the morning walks
separating Malecon from the sea.
I watched the waves
cover the tiny sandy beach,
then dash against green, mossy rocks.
At night, I watched, with delight,
the moon's dance on the sea's surface.
And beneath the wall,
sewers crawled under heavy rocks.

Then the children came
and belly-flopped into deep pools
where they splashed about and swam
in a profusion of joy.

It was in the apex of the pleasure dome
that I found Berta:
dark in complexion, eyes, and hair,
gifted in bodily symmetry
and cultivated in the arts
of erotic rapture.
I hailed her as a goddess
who heard my prayer
for joyful deliverance,
and I offered her thanks
for her heavenly embrace.

The cathedral before departure
was also a novel experience:
as soon as I entered the church,
the street noise grew silent
as the commerce of my ego vanished;
I could feel a greater-than-human force
gripping my soul
for where I sat
was a slice of sacred space.

First Hangover, 1950

The scene shifts in this poem from Florida and Cuba to Washington Square College, New York University, where I was living in Greenwich Village. One of my favorite teachers was Delmore Schwartz, a poet, who taught aesthetics in the Department of Philosophy. It was he who introduced me and other students to the Ninety-second Street YMHA where the great poets of the time read from their work. A favorite of Schwartz was Dylan Thomas, who was an alcoholic. We were taken, on occasion, to a bar called the White Horse Tavern on Hudson Street. Naturally, I aped the master poets and did experience a hangover.

The wetness disgusts me now
as most things do.
I want to shatter the window pane,
then spit on a leaf.
I want to feel fire on my fingernails
and scream through my nose.
Oh, to bury the snake
I slashed to death
in my sleep.
Oh, sleep, a lost delicacy,
though hardly forgotten.
I want to streak nudely
along the moist, infectious street,
shouting invectives
at the all-pervading spirit.
I am the thinker and the doer,
the all-feeling blank,
relishing the slippery sounds of silence.
Will the morning
awaken me in a bath of sunlight
or will my morning
collapse at midnight?

Early Morn at Summer Camp, 1950

Nature, as seen in this poem, was another side of my personal life at the time.

We strolled the night
amid stately trees in hushed columns.
Then a clearing appeared,
and we knew the lake was near.
At my feet at the water's edge,
a warty toad started leaping.
We heard a frog and crickets
in a nocturnal ensemble.
Then up above,
rays of light crept about
in the starry sky.
Black mounds, only vaguely discerned,
now changed into green hills
surrounded by mist
in a mystic wonderland.
We watched a purple sky
dipped in pools of red
silently descend the distant slopes.
We humble humans
stood awe-struck
before an ever-changing world
beyond our grasp.
Then, as time passed,
and the sun embraced us,
we heard birds warble
in a staghorn sumac.
And when the forest was suddenly ablaze
from the fire of the sun,
gold-colored flowers
lined the widening trail
as far as the eyes could see.

A Summer View from the Summit of Garret Mountain, 1950

In this second poem on "nature," written in my home town of Paterson, New Jersey, I am enjoying the surroundings of Garret Mountain, which overlooks the city. According to my diary, I was influenced at the time by William Carlos Williams, who in 1950 won the National Book Award for his volume of poetry on Paterson. *I had first met Williams during one of his readings at the Ninety-second Street Y.*

Not a breathless moment
on the winding trail
scaling Garret Mountain
in the heat of summer.
I have long since
left behind, momentarily,
earthly sounds, sights and smells.
From where I sit,
the oncoming train
is but a miniature toy.
My world of vision
is panoramic now:
surrounding the city
are fields, farms, and a flood of forest;
and above, misty bags of silvery fluff
move across space with snail-like progress.
No trafficking of cars up here;
only birds darken a patch of sky
in their flight southward.
Oh, sweet silence,
transcending the cares of the ego
to refresh my inner spirit.

Autumn Scene, 1950

This is the third of the impressionistic nature poems from 1950.

Green leaves are fewer
along the winding trail.
On either side,
the façade of trees
are a spectrum of colors.
Why this natural splash of radiance
before the wintry demise?
Soon the colors will fade
and the leaves will scatter in the wind.
We are all victims of history
as the cycles spin endlessly.
But, for now, I shall take joy
in the streaky, pale, orange sky.
Soon it, too, will succumb
to the oncoming veil of darkness.
The trail leads in both directions at once:
the final surge of summer
and the sureness of death's dominion.

From Our Apartment Window on Ho Chi Minh Serani, 1961

This is the first poem on impressions of Calcutta during a first trip there to do research on my doctoral dissertation. I had a Ford Foundation Area Fellowship, and my wife and I lived in an apartment house on the same street as the representative office of the American Embassy.

The fast-moving clouds
are dark with monsoon rain.
The black-skinned Madrasi,
in his bearer's white,
prepares to serve a meal.
The Marawari papa and son
are in a heated debate
while leaning over the balcony.
A fat, short-haired cat
yawns from behind a screened window,
then winds its legs about its neck
with yoga-like nimbleness.
The incessant noise of crows
falls strangely silent
as the long day unravels,
and the feeble-colored sunset
spreads across the sky.

Then as the earth
is bathed in the first wave of darkness,
fresh sounds are carried in a soft, tropical breeze:
a woman with a stringed instrument
is singing a lyric
in praise of Krishna;
there is also a noisy cacophony
as pots and pans
are led to the wash;
the menacing bark
of a homeless dog
in search of food;
two cars gathering speed

somewhere on Ho Chi Minh Serani,
where even in the late hours,
shoppers throng.

A darkened room across the yard
is suddenly candle-lit,
and seated alone,
is a sari-clad, dark-haired woman
sipping cognac.

Return to Calcutta, 1962

This second poem on Calcutta after I returned from a trip to Southeast Asia is perhaps less impressionistic and more philosophical. Whatever else we came to feel about Calcutta, it had become a second home for my wife and myself. For me, it was the intellectual quality of Bengali culture and the city that I appreciated most of all.

I returned
to my adopted
Eastern Gangetic home
on a ship then leaving
that cargoed
thousands of tons
of betel nut.
Red spit
would now fly
from double-deckered buses
on Chouringhee,
and the city
would be painted red
in a fortnight.
Oh, city
of palaces, graft, corruption
and the corporation;
city of tubercular rickshawwallahs
and of gutters
straddled by men
busily easing themselves;
city of
the legless, armless
and homeless dregs.
Look to Howrah Bridge
that spans
the holiest of rivers,
and across the bridge
where oxen-men
carry the weight of commerce
on their backs.

The black face of Calcutta
sweats from endless toil
and insufferable heat.
The white face of Calcutta
stands aloof
from the crowd,
and nourishes itself
on its own members
who sit
in palatial homes
cultivating
the art of idleness.
It was good seeing the sacred cows
moving like pedestrians,
on all fours,
them leaving
their unprinted fecal calling cards.
It was good, once more,
to feed
on the Bengali intellect.
We are home, at last.
Though the sky is gray,
the monsoon rains have tapered off.
Cannot winter
be lurking close behind?

Dedicated to My Friend Who Pocketed Ashtrays, 1973

I did have a friend who pocketed ashtrays, but his name was not Joshua. I might point out that this poem was also intended to offer the would-be traveler to Europe a possible tour.

My former friend, Joshua,
lived a dull life
except that he enjoyed
swiping ashtrays
while vacationing in Europe.
His home was a museum
and a virtual Madison Avenue,
in miniature,
of free publicity.
Air France was shaped
like a blue vagina
with the cigarette
an innocent intruder.
The Guinness,
lifted from a sidewalk café,
had the hungry look
of a carnivorous jungle plant
devouring many a butt
from nimble-fingered smokers.
During a nervous moment
in a German gasthouse,
he had pilfered
a huge, ruby-colored
and heart-shaped Zuban.
In Rome,
while clerks of Air Italia
were momentarily diverted
over a rain cancellation,
a gem-like replica of St. Peter
was stuffed into his pocket.
A castle with moat
from the chateaux country
with a Napoleon cognac label,

disappeared, one evening,
from a brasserie in a French village.
There were other souvenirs:
a consolation prize
from a Riviera casino
after a bad night at roulette;
a deep-yellow El Greco-type elongation
from Lugano;
a miniature, purple, potted plant
from Prague.
And so my sensuous friend
lived in his pleasure dome,
leaving behind momentos of ash,
as he circled the room
on his sojourn of Europe.

My Friend's Cabin, 1975

This poem contains my impressions of a very special cabin belonging to a very special friend located on a lake north of Minneapolis.

A cabin is a cabin is a cabin
(pure image devoid of meaning and mystery).
For a cabin
is also a symbol.
My friend's cabin
is a nest
where birds
nourish their young:
nature walks, frank talks,
closeness under the elms;
familial memories deliciously sentimental;
blood ties made fast
by intimately shared experiences.
My friend's cabin
is a web
of romantic entanglements
with a lake,
a Venetian canal,
under a full moon
and the music of sweet sensuality
played to the rapturous notes
on Krishna's flute.
My friend's cabin
is a cave
where creative man,
limited, but free,
reaches out
for the Platonic idea,
undefiled by earthiness;
not the creativity
of the womb
but the shimmering light
of musical abstraction;

the keyboard, the mind and the fingers,
transcend life and death,
in a rational orgy
of the disembodied
and bloodless composition.
My friend's cabin
is an ashram
where the world-weary spirit
reemerges in refuge;
yellow leaves of silvery birches
glisten in the autumn sun;
the sunsets across the lake
are subsumed silently
by fisherfolk
in a slow-moving craft;
it is all like
a divine campus
within a Blakeian vision.

Sewer City Is in Everyland, 1976

The impressions presented here are of a place which may not actually exist but they are familiar to all of us nevertheless.

The gray flannel
or olive tweed
of repressionville,
vacations in Sewer City
where once a year,
John Sneed
can play the drunken sailor.

Sewer City offers
a web of illusion:
every hash house
is a gourmet palace;
every torso
is the shapely object
of a wet dream
out of Hollywood;
every smoke-stenched casino
is Monte Carlo.

On the beach,
the slabs
of white flesh
are blackened
by the rays
of a burning, celestial
ball of fire.

Twilight,
on Sewer City beach,
is for promenade:
sparrow-breasted girls
in shorts
stroll in pairs,

chattering and chuckling
with a steady eye
for the opposite sex;
sixty-year-old women
yearn to regain thirty,
when their bodies
were still magnets
to attract
the male beast.

Lonely men
from repressionville
prowl the streets
obliterating
their olive green lives
with gallons
of alcoholic brew.
They become
faceless men
when encountering
the skirt-lifting
flesh sellers.

Then,
when the early morning hours
overtake vacationland,
and silence
is king,
the ego
of everyman
in Everyland,
is laid to rest.

Episode on the Bangladeshi Riviera, 1976

These impressions were gathered while on my final vacation in Bangladesh after a year at Rajshahi University as a visiting South Asia historian from the United States.

I sit alone,
in a cave
on the beach
at Cox's Bazaar
on the Bay of Bengal.
In front,
whitecaps on a blue sea,
and above,
a darkening gray sky.
On the shoreline,
beyond the long stretch
of sand,
contoured hillcocks
protrude southward.
I switch my head
seaward
to follow
a solitary shark sail
maneuvering between the waves,
then disappear.
I turn my face,
and feel
a delicate breeze,
then gaze upward
to follow the path
of the wispy clouds.
My hotel is tourist-intended,
but, at present,
tourist free.
I am the solitary guest.
The restaurant menu
for tonight
is wishful thinking

for the Bangladeshi chef.
The last time
he served an American steak
was under
Ayub Khan's dictatorship.
I shall eat
my mysterious masala
while watching
the mist rise
above the beach.

A Snail's Pace in a Snail's World on a Sandy Beach, 1978

Though I do not recall which beach I was visiting at the time, I do remember my interest in micro-cosms.

Widening beach at low tide;
soft-sounding whitecaps
breaking gently;
sky and surf
merge in
the dense fog.
Footprints
mark a trail
along the wet sand:
each print
encompasses
a busy snail's world;
delicate lines
etched by
an invisible hand
writing
indecipherable hieroglyphics
in the sand,
an aesthetic of spontaneity
like the random
splashing of paints.
Our footprints
representing
a myriad of designs,
intrude themselves
into snail's space;
and can it be said
a snail's pace
is as imperceptible
as human progress.
The hours collapse
into high tide;
each print

is washed clean
of movement
and the delicacy
of life.

On Turning Fifty, 1980

To this very day, I cannot say that birthdays have brought out anything bordering on wisdom or profundity. I remember during one birthday, not long ago, that what I wanted most was to become my own best friend.

Has each of us
lived alone so long
that we are beyond
the point of no return?
Flashes of remembrance
come and go;
lush memories of love and sex
appear and reappear
amid a cathedral worth of passion.
I still yearn
for blossoms at springtime.
I have endured
my share
of self-reproach
after years of alienation
from the Judeo-Christian ethic.
It has taken
fifty years
to engineer
that reservoir of suspicion
against my roots,
and live with it.
Of immense disappointment,
at fifty,
is the continued imprisonment
of my true self:
my ego,
chained to the world of illusion,
still remains
king of the hill.

Images from Hiking on Signal Mountain on the Irish West Coast, 1994

These impressions are from one of my many hiking trips which have taken me to different parts of the world. Only recently, have I tried to record these journeys in some poetic form.

Shades of green
in the distance,
resemble a waterfall
of liquid earth
rolling down
the mountain side.

Climbers walking the world
follow sheep-dip trails
that weave sideways,
or rise abruptly,
in the steep and
narrow grass lanes.

The hikers
stir the sheep
out of their
complacent inertia,
and send them
into retreat
to the man-made
walls of rock.

Dark, barren cliffs,
too often hidden
in the impenetrable
Irish mist,
are today,
clear and bright islands
in the sun.

No shadows streak
across the hilly slopes;
the sky is cloudless,
the ocean still.
And the sounds
of the seagulls
are a pleasant music,
arousing a delicious serenity
that we feel
when all is right
with the world.

Prague Impressions, 2003

These poetic impressions of Prague were written after I recovered from an exhausting hiking trip from Vienna to Prague.

Just paces
from Kafka's former domicile,
multi-lingual lyrics
are flowing
above the square
from a yellow-shirted
Norwegian chorus.
A Disney-like golem
amid holocaust survivals,
lies in waiting
by a graveyard
where broken lives
lay squandered
in a timeless vacuum,
and stone-carved etchings
are bright
in the noonday sun.

A white-haired saxophonist
is swinging cool notes
on Charles Bridge.

Then ambling
through a myriad
of narrow streets and lanes,
ever climbing
to the castle above
to see
the changing of the guard.
The gardens
are, in the twilight,
but a
color-streaked memory.

Night has fallen,
while we are gently adrift
on the river,
gliding without purpose
as in the stream of life.
We seem momentarily lost
in a dream-like web
of shadows,
but the mood explodes
from Dixie sounds of ragtime
in a nearby boat.
We strain
to relish the jazz;
the beautiful voice
of Pearl Bailey,
so hauntingly memorable
along the moonlit channel,
is slowly swallowed
in silent space
until she can be heard
no more.

Impressions of Cinque Terre, 2003

Cinque Terre, one of the most beautiful places I have traveled on earth, was also among the most difficult terrains I have ever hiked. It may have been so because I was seventy-three years of age when I did so with a group of much younger hikers.

In the past,
before the Romans,
trails across
rugged mountains
in Cinque Terre,
linked otherwise
inaccessible towns
in this breathtaking slice
of coastal beauty
on the Italian Mediterranean.
Centuries passed,
between then and now,
and however
inhospitable to
human habitation,
people settled
and survived
the terrain.
Soon, towering fortresses
graced the mountain ridges
to keep off
marauding pirates
bent on women and treasure.
And nearby,
another protective structure
came forth:
a Romanesque church,
the sacred circle
in a profane world,
offering brief respite
to weary travelers
stumbling along
the rocky road
of existence.

Cultural Insights and Images

ꕥ

Maya Leads Me by the Nose, 1957

The poems in this section are mainly about travel, but unlike the poetry in the first section, these reflect a deeper personal and intellectual experience associated with a given place. In the first section, I am gathering impressions on what the world is like. Even as a graduate student seriously at work on a project in India, much of what I see around me is through the eyes of a tourist. But, in time, I develop a certain relationship with cultures, which enables me to characterize them in terms of special interests. In "Maya Leads Me By the Nose," for example, I am not gathering impressions for a travelogue on the French Riviera, but rather I utilize France as a special place in the hearts of former soldiers such as my father-in-law and myself.

My father-in-law, Stanley,
battled the Huns in 1917,
and carries a myth
in his heart:
he once found peace,
in war,
in the French village
of Couverpuites,
when he knelt
beside a French girl
in an old church
and joined her in prayer.
The village still stands,
as does the timeless church,
but the girl
is now a name
barely seen
on a stone
in the churchyard.
Their experience
is today
but a fragile memory.
Lives perish with ease
but only myths
die hard.

Once, I came to Nice,
on the French Riviera,
a soldier, also,
in search
of a lost identity.
For a week,
I was lost in wine,
lost in flesh,
lost in the carnival crowds
on a brisk February day,
and lost in timelessness.
While boozing till dawn
at Albert's,
I watched the yellow disc
rise above
the blue sea and the green mountains.

I am in Nice, once more,
now with wife and in-laws,
in the same hotel,
the same Promenade des Anglais,
and the same
bikinis and tight skirts,
Niçoise salad and vin ordinaire,
and the same oyster soup
at Chat Noir.
But the restless,
indefinable yearning
for lostness is gone,
and Maya
leads me by the nose.

The Tourist Who Captured a Soul, 1962

This poem was written during a vacation from India. My wife and I visited a cemetery, among other places, in Malacca, Malaysia, and it was the constant picture-taking by tourists which gave me the idea for this piece.

In Malacca,
on a rolling hill
facing the Straits,
there is found
a sprawling Chinese cemetery,
the oldest in Malaysia.
The Portuguese came as noisy invaders,
then the Dutch,
then the English;
but quiet prevailed
on the hillside
where the souls of the dead
rested, unmolested.

After the English,
the tourists
filtered in,
and an aging Chinese priest
built himself a temple
which like a bastion,
stood between clicking cameras
and desecration.

One day,
when the sun stood high
in the mid-day sky,
and the gulls flew about
in great profusion,
a solitary tourist
strolled between the lonely graves
with a Leica
suspended from narrow shoulders,

awaiting inner commands
to fire upon the world
and capture
everything in sight.

That afternoon,
when he raised his camera
to his squinting good eye,
one grave stood out;
he clicked quickly.
The camera shook violently
and a groan
split the air.
With trembling fingers,
he opened the fancy box
(exposing a half roll of film).
A foul breath of air
passed his nostrils
smelling as putrid
as death itself.

Near the temple,
sat the priest
in smug silence
wearing the face
of a smiling Buddha.

Globalization in Southeast Asia, 1962 (1963)

I am amazed at how well I predicted the triumph of globalization in this part of Asia. I am also intrigued on how much I appreciated the process then as against my present attitude.

In Bangkok,
the sexy masseuse
is the queen of porn,
while your brightly-clad
and clean-shaven monks
abandon Buddha
for the shores of the American ego.
In Saigon,
the Parisian sidewalk cafés
are deserted now,
but for those who sip their pernod
without fear of communist bombs.
Djakarta, dominating 3,000 islands
in the name of Indonesia,
seeks to maintain
the illusion of unity
amid a cluster
of peoples and tongues.
Can it be
that stable statehood
may be drowning
in the angry sea
of worthless paper called currency?
Meanwhile, the enchanted Hindu Bali
has lost its magic
to Aussie tourists on motorbikes.
Then there are the Chinese,
or the Jews of Southeast Asia,
who wear a haggard frown
when deported from Indonesia.
Though in Hong Kong and Singapore,
the Chinese entrepreneur prevails,
having mastered the lore
of his British custodian.

The tides of change
are sweeping across the region
with a new religion
aping western progress:
human-drawn rickshaws
are as dated
as pig-tailed Chinamen and Fu Manchu;
the myth of the unchanging East
is a smoke-screen to conceal ethnocentrism;
but the smoke is clearing.
That wall of myth
separating East from West,
is being blown away
by cyclonic gusts
of fresh metaphoric winds.

The Great Benares Circus, 1962

I hope the reader can now understand how poems such as this one are quite different from the first set. This poem in no way is meant to entice the tourist with impressions of Hinduism's holiest city. When I reread this poem, in light of what I wrote in the previous one, I would be most interested in returning to Banares to assess the impact of globalization.

Even when Nehru speechifies
on India's modernization,
Benares remains
South Asia's
great circus town.
The sharp nail beds
have passed
from the banks of the Ganges,
but the show
is still enough of a hair-raiser
to provide surviving creatures
of an exotic past.

The ghats
are a colorful spectacle
in the early morning sun.
Upon steps
as old as eternity,
exposed flesh
by the hundreds,
walk to the water's edge
and immerse themselves
in Ganga's bosom.
Then, once more,
out of the water
and into the scorching sun,
they sigh with relief
as sins, like scum,
vanish in the foamy flow.

And above the steps,
saddhus sit
cross-legged and wise,
with their white beards
and piercing eyes.

Nearby,
stands a small Hindu temple,
its tile floors
stained with pan, crushed marigolds
and cow's excrement;
a mob of worshippers
moves round and round
a stone-mute god.

And down the steps
at the river's edge,
crossed-legged and cross-sexed,
sari-clad men
dangle their keys,
singing their praises
of the lord.

At the burning ghat,
where the dead are given
their final farewell,
a protruding foot
has been slow to burn,
and when the wind shifts,
thoughts are carried
to a backyard barbecue.

Then a cluster
of the elderly,
at death's door,
encircles the kirtan singers
bellowing lyrics
to the pounding rhythm.

The winding lanes
of Benares
seal off time,
as the hordes of mendicants
implore a medieval god
to restore the values
of a mythic age.
Scores of Hindu women
bargain for Siva's penis in stone
and a potful of Ganges water.

With the setting sun,
the dancing has ceased
and the saintly deaf mute
no longer shakes,
but has dozed off
in a squat.

The Pink City of Jaipur, 1963

This poem was written after my first visit to a Rajput city, and I must confess that it is as much tourist-oriented, as with the poetry in section one, as it is designed to express something creative, historically significant and meaningful about Jaipur.

In a valley
amid the Rajasthani hills,
lies a maharaja's city
as pink and symmetrical
as a celluloid fantasyland.
Long ago and today,
castles reach above
the parched land
on all sides.
Once upon a time,
in the feudal age of Rajputs,
knights were bold
and widows ascended flaming pyres
to join their husbands
in the hereafter.
From a slit
in a castle wall,
one can see
an ageless caravan
of slow-paced camels
with an elegant stride.
They disappear
in the west
where the rocky earth crumbles
into the hot, yellow, desert sands.
Jaipur's streets
are as wide as modernity,
but the traffic
is as ancient as Jerusalem.
Auspicious wedding processions
clog the streets
either on lavishly-bedecked horses
or towering, painted elephants.

The markets are teeming this day
with Marawari women
in bright-colored saris
ornamented with gold and silver.
Hundreds of noisy birds
sit on wires
ready to pounce
on scattered seed.
Rajput men
also roam the streets
clad in orange, red and yellow turbans,
adding to the dazzling impact
of sharp colors
under a brilliant sun.
Then when daylight
begins to ebb,
and the tide of darkness
sweeps over the land,
tongas look like chariots
while the lighted castles
ignite historic memories
of a bygone age.

Kibbutz, 1963

As the final lines of the poem suggest, Israel may change from what it was back in the 1960s to what it is today, whatever that happens to be. The kibbutz was a microcosm of what the people of Israel had achieved. Of course, generational changes are inevitable, but, as with many other people visiting Israel at the time, I wanted to express my admiration for the realization of the idea of kibbutz.

The Austrian Jew
shepherds his restless flock
across the lush,
sloping meadow.
Soon,
he will rest
and his eyes,
growing moist,
will sweep across
this biblical land.
Within his lifetime,
the parched earth
turned green,
yielding crops
like a radish
the size of a boxer's fist,
and a lemon
as large as a grapefruit;
all cultivated
by city Jews
who had never smelled manure.

A German Jewess
who had fled to China in 1938,
moved, once more,
a decade later,
to the new Israeli state.
A scarfaced Polish Jew
had survived Auschwitz
with a dream:

he would cross Europe
to the land of Zion.
The strong-bodied American Jew
had already farmed
(in Iowa)
before carrying his will and skill
to the shores of Israel.

They all live as one
in a non-coercive communism,
where none is richer
than his neighbor,
and all net earnings
are diverted into collective use.
Here are schools
where grades are unknown
and achievement gauged
without competitive trappings.
For those
who inherit this miracle,
this question:
is the kibbutz
an exotic plant
due for extinction
by the human condition?

Iran, 1963

This poem constitutes my effort at integrating a historic vision of Iran, both Islamic and classical, with a renaissance view of its future as imbibing the modernistic spirit but without losing its cultural identity. My wife and I visited Persepolis, the city which represented the classical golden age; then Isfahan, the city which was the high point of its Islamic era; and then Teheran where we found ample evidence of modernism.

Black gold
has built
a city of bourgeoisie palaces
in the showcase
of Teheran.
The privileged few
seem content
to keep
the twentieth-century revolutions
confined
within their own circle.
There is the Shah,
physician of his people,
who fears
the epidemic of violence
when the red microbe
will permeate
the countryside.
The landed gentry
must feel
the whip of progress,
as must the mullahs
who have
suppressed women
far too long.

Far back,
Persia was a civilization
to be reckoned with;
Persepolis
was the Paris or London
of the ancient world
while the emperors,
Darius and Xerxes,
towered above their peers,
as did Asoka of India
and Caesar of Rome.

But empires erode
as frontiers shift
and barbarians
grow restless.
Blood flows
as cities crumble.
Then cultures
grow war-weary,
dying under
the thundering horses
and barbaric warriors
with slashing blades.
Thus did Alexander
obliterate Persepolis,
while the Arab zealots
entombed classical Persia,
supplanting
a diversity of creative expression
with a single-minded devotion
to faith.

Iran's hope
is in her renaissance:
she must choose
between Islam
and her Persian heritage.
Iran must transcend
the darkness
of her Middle Ages.
A new generation
must celebrate
Persia's golden age
when Cyrus
freed the Jews
from their captivity
in Babylon,
and the empire
reached from Egypt to India,
and the Greeks of Ionia
brought wealth
in trade,
and Zoroaster
offered salvation
to a violent world
in transition.
The glories
of ancient Persia
may well be
Iran's guide
to a new identity
in the modern world.
Why must the soil
of the nation
remain arid
for want
of a new spirit?

April in Paris, 1963

As in other poems in this section, travel is not simply distracting oneself at foreign ports of call, but is a means of acquiring deeper meanings of self-understanding. Also, since we change historically as everything else does, each return to Paris reveals some aspect of the change.

We all return to Paris
sooner or later,
and bemoan our spent youth.

Seeing Paris the first time,
is like a first reading
of Thomas Wolfe.

To the young mind
of the incurable romantic,
each café
is a concert hall
of conversational chamber music,
and the intimacy
is brilliant but cozy.

Then, I walked the narrow streets
of the Left Bank,
imagining myself
brushing against
Hemingway, Stein, or Fitzgerald.

After April, at Luxemburg,
the flowers are in bloom,
and it is easy
to ignore the black grime
of the Louvre.

The first time,
I was a soldier
on leave in Paris,
and each exploit in Pigalle
was an explosion of sensual fantasy.

Except for an enchanting dinner
at La Perouse,
the gourmet within
was of little import.

It was far better
to devour a sunset
from a bridge on the Seine,
or a weird splash
of colors on a canvas.

Now Paris and I
have both changed.
It is in the omelet's taste
and not the sights and smells
about the café,
which excite me.

And in the cafés
where once a Sartre
expounded truth,
the fat people now repose.

Paris, this April,
is an extension of March:
Chicago's wind
and London's damp,
are inescapable.

Once, I avoided drunken brawls
on Place Pigalle,
but today,
I creep about
in a herd of onlookers.

Where are the sounds today
of white musicians
playing black jazz?
There are more galleries
but fewer artists.

Then and now,
thank the Lord,
there is Notre Dame
where I find peace
in a dark corner,
surrounded by a world
of gothic rapture.

Ah, to Be in England in the Spring of 1963

I find it intriguing that, though I have been to London more often than to Paris—mainly for scholarly research—my treatment of Paris in the previous poem is historical whereas this poem on England is ahistorical. To this day, I seem more interested in capturing cultural images of England than using the British experience to deepen self-understanding.

Ah, to be in England
now that spring is here.
Though the air is damp
and the clouds
a durable fixture
in the English heavens,
an ecstasy of colors
peers through
the monochromatic
English mist,
pleasing the hearts
of stoic Britons.
A procession
of cherry blossoms
winds its way
along the Thames
to London town.
We stroll along
the jungle of rhododendrans
in Kew Gardens,
and the tulips
at Hampton and Windsor,
amid the emerald green.

Ah, to be in England
where sturdy,
apple-cheeked
arthritic bodies,
thaw out
after a long winter.
Huddled together

for warmth
in hotel rooms
as drafty as castles,
we watch
the metered, heater boxes
swallow
a plethora of shillings.
The hard winter
is over;
now the Englishman
can wipe away
the ice
from his mustache
and heckle
his centrally heated
American cousin
for recklessly indulging himself.

Ah, to be in England
now that spring is here.
The cold-weather
trickle of trouists
increases by stages
until the July deluge
when the gates
of Buckingham Palace
are stormed daily,
and a million eyes
in a single summer
shudder at the chopper
in London Tower.
Ach, to be in England.
Who needs it?

Twelve Views of Bharat (India), 1964

This poem was written a year after returning from India. Like the previous poem on England, I am attempting to depict a culture as I see it. Interestingly, my passion for expression on India was seldom aimed at self-understanding in any psychological sense as it was cultural understanding in an anthropological sense.

The sannyasi
cleans his nose
with the holy Gangetic water
near the burning ghats
of Benares.

The Calcutta student
looks lean and hungry
as he applies a torch
to a tram
in the midst of a riot.

Paintings
of Rammohun, Tagore, and Ramakrishna
are omnipresent
on the living room walls
of bhadralok Bengali households.

A full-page ad
in the press,
paid for
by Tata and Birla,
urges Indians
to follow Nehru
on the road to socialism.

India is a nation
where caste
is a crime
punishable
by harsh, vindictive language.

Child brides
may soon be history,
not for the crime
it surely is in India,
but for TV's global reach.

It is common
to be the recipient
of the twin odors:
exotically-seasoned Indian food
and the smell of hot dung cakes
in a poorly-ventilated room.

I still harbor the image
of a Bihari
pulling a rickshaw
over the steamy Calcutta pavement.

The horde of beggars
at the hotel entrance
confronts tourists
with the refrain:
"no mama, no papa, no sister, no brother."

The swollen bellies
of Indian women
could repopulate
the city of New York
in a single year.

The Indian nation
is a unity
in diversity;
but Tamil Nadu, Bengal
and the Punjab
spell diversity
in the apparent unity.

When the Indian children
splash about
in the monsoon rain,
can winter be far behind?

Caricature and National Identity in the 1960s: India and Israel, 1964

Initially, this poem was a comparative attempt to separate stereotype from cultural reality in Israel and India, but in retrospect, it constitutes a prophecy of a sort on the future of these two new nations. In 1964, after a year away from both countries, I could see what we call globalization on the horizon of their futures. Moreover, I find it interesting that I was more sympathetic to this trend than I am today.

If you stand
along the Mea Searim,
in Jerusalem,
on Purim night,
it is like the ghetto
in Lithuania
centuries back.
Around you,
under fur hats,
long-bearded men
in long, black coats
dance with mystic frenzy
and sing holy lyrics
from a timeless past.
There are also boys
with beardless faces
wearing curls
and the black satin
of their elders.
Their rabbi declares,
"We are the real Jews."
Does a real Jew
put the vellum on
each day
or wear a yamuka
on the street?
Is this a real Jew
or a medieval caricature?

The world is full
of such misapprehensions:
it sees the wild look
of an Indian saddhu,
or glances
at the devout Hindu peasant
who applies orange paint
to the Lord's image
on the eve
of Siva ratre.
The world concludes
these caricatures
are the true Hindu identity.

Is orthodoxy
the true banner
of Israeli Judaism?
What can a boy do
when from infancy,
the Talmud
is thrust before him
as the main avenue
to knowledge and wisdom?
Was the inspiration
that guided
the citizen soldiers
to wrest Jerusalem
from Arab hands,
born while seated
at prayer
in the Talmud Torah?
Israel is now
a new state
and a new state of being:
Jews elect Jews
to public office,
drive trucks
and probe space;

they also till the soil
with the same skills
as an Iowa farmer.

And what of the land
with the atom bomb
where snake charmers abide
and holy men meditate
on a bed of nails?
Which god
does India worship today:
the avatar, Lord Krishna,
or computer science?

War and Genocide Across the Border in Bangladesh, 1971

I was in Calcutta once again in 1969 to 1971 on an American Institute of Indian Studies Fellowship to do research for another monograph dealing with the Brahmo Samaj and the Shaping of the Modern Indian Mind. In 1971, violence erupted across the border in East Pakistan which led to a war of independence by the Bengalis there and to genocide of the same people by the army of West Pakistan. Much of what happened is contained in a novel I wrote later entitled Scratches on Kali's Mind.

Time is running out
across the border;
people are squatting
on the edge of doom;
sonar Bangla
at the gate
of inferno
awaiting her baptism
in the blood
of martyrs.
Why do I seek
the world of the dead
in dust-filled archives?
The corridors
in which I wander
are hotels
for white ants.
Here I sit,
pontificating
the ridiculous and sublime:
thoughts of scholarship
and thoughts of Listerine;
the somber purity
of questing truth
and the frivolity
of light-hearted discourse.
I shall booze away
East Pakistan's murderous closure:
both immediate horrors
and the dreaded secrets
of what is yet to come.

The Man Who Chased Sunsets with His Camera, 1971

This poem was written while sipping wine at a hotel restaurant in Singapore. It is very much autobiographical since I was most enamored with sunsets— especially those on a body of water from somewhere on the shoreline.

Waiting patiently
on a bridge
spanning the Parisian Seine;
standing on deck
lusting the dip of the sun
from Naples to Capri;
island hopping the Aegean
to pursue the golden rays
in their final glory;
squatting on Malabar Hill
to watch a scorching sun
redden the sky;
climbing a Hong Kong peak
for a lingering view
of an island
engulfed by the frenzy
of radiant color.

Sadly, the Kodachromes
would not respond,
and the man felt
he had chased a dream
and not a sunset.

In Paris,
an overenthusiastic aperture opening
transformed the sunset
into a yellow mist;
a choppy sea in Capri
doubled the image;
In Mykonos,
he had waited
moments too long

and the slide
was sunless
and pitch black;
the scorching Indian sun,
at Malabar,
emerged as specs of yellow dust
in narrow streaks
sitting on a platform
of sea.

But in Hong Kong,
a near replica of nature
was salvaged
and the man marvelled
at the splendor
of color.

Taj Mahal: Visit to a Martyr's Tomb, 1980

I was in India on a Guggenheim grant when I took my kids to their first visit of India's most popular historical monument, the Taj Mahal. Though I had been to the Taj twice before, I never thought about a poetic effort to assess it historically, until after the visit with my son and daughter.

It is said Shah Jahan never ceased to love his wife
in death, as in life.
So he erected the Taj Mahal
as a lasting tribute to his eternal beloved.
But, did not the wife of Shah Jahan
die a martyr's death?

Here was a woman
who gave birth fourteen times
in fifteen years of wedded "bliss".
Death may have come to her
as a lover, also.
Was not the promise of heaven
as a sweet-aromatic paradise
still one more seduction?
Death may also have come to her as a father
to seal again her virginal flower.

What finer choice than white marble
to restore the state of the unmolested virgin?
How the marble shines in the noonday sun!
I have been a frequent visitor of the Taj when the moon is full
and the dome, bathed in a flood of light,
rises above the dusty mist.
Now husband and wife lie together,
and tourists flock from all corners of the earth
to pay homage to the Mughal couple.

Casablanca, 1994

I was actually in Morocco when this poem was written and had visited Casablanca a few days earlier. I have no idea what brought on the mood that seems to permeate each line of the poetry.

Where on earth
am I to meet you,
accidentally, on purpose?
Though the time
has been short,
I weary of my residence
in Casablanca.
Here, I have imprisoned my affection
and cultivated my love
in a stony field.
In my Casablanca,
there is neither fruit nor flowers;
and I have yet to feel raindrops
in this land
where there are only clouds
of yellow dust.

Icelandic Images, 1997

This poem written on a plane after a hiking trip with geologists in Iceland, may seem better suited in section one dealing with impressions of a country. But, in fact, as my geologist friends observed, it could only have been written by a historian of human societies rather than one largely concerned with the history of other natural conglomerations, such as rocks. Also, I am rather proud of my last stanza in consideration of the recent disaster of epic proportions in the Indian Ocean which took over 200,000 lives.

The rock,
not the human,
is the microcosm
of the Icelandic universe.
There is geological time
but no consciousness
of the passage of time.
The footsteps
of human history
have left hardly a trace
in this nature-inspired
dialectic
between fire and ice.
Before the Vikings,
Iceland was
other—planetary
in its absence
of human chatter
and design.
It was a world
of endless horizons
uncorrupted
by human cities, crops and wars.

We cruise
along glacier lakes,
enraptured
by this ever-changing
exotic moonscape
with iceberg islands
floating around us.

It is a land
of 10,000 waterfalls,
with sheep
seeking greener pastures
at 2,000 feet.
And there is Mt. Hekla,
mysterious, smoldering,
mist-encircled crater,
where Lucifer holds court
(or so the popes believed).

Iceland is nature's dominion,
not ours;
and being so,
the earth trembles
in the wake
of God's wrath.
For nature, too,
wears the masks
of Robespierre and Lenin:
exploding mountains
and the quaking ground
give testimony
to Nature's reign of terror.

Milan in the Age of Globalization, 2003

I had wanted originally to do an impressionistic, tourist-oriented poem on Milan, but when I sat down to write it, something very different emerged.

The taste of American pizza
on the streets
of the city;
bald-headed adolescents
(Venturas with earings);
blonde-haired Italians
in tight-ass
and tight-crotch
jeans;
avenues and alleys
littered
with plastic garbage.
The obese
in mind and spirit
occupying
the fast-food palaces
in Fat City.
And everywhere,
the stench
of consumed tobacco,
as curls
of contaminated smoke
rise
from parted lips.

Thoughts of Death and Dying on a Rhone River Cruise, 2003

This poem was written on a cruise that took us to such places on the Rhone River as Lyon, Avignon, and Arles.

My former lover
has been
my companion
on a cruise
along the Rhone.
Can a friendship
be born
out of
a dying relationship?
We feel
quite at home
among the Roman ruins.
And like the Roman hearts
in the river towns,
our love is history.
Our lives
seem to flow
like the river
collecting the debris
of hopeful dreams
and hopeless dilemmas.
And like the river,
we exit into the sea
leaving behind
the riddle
of our existence.

Mazatlan, 2003

I confronted globalization a second time here in Mexico along the Pacific coast. I had been exploring the possibility of a winter retreat.

Tourist terrain,
where the economy
is greased
by the Yankee dollar.
The flesh of traditions
is being devoured
by carnivorous
self-gratification.
Alien retirees
flock here
in droves
to consume
the warmth and leisure
of predictable
sunlit days.
El Cid
is the paradigm
of the retiree's
ecological niche:
a golf course
at your doorstep
and friendly bars
where oblivion
is greeted nightly.
The greatest casualty
is the Mexican culture;
Mickey Mouse
has found
a congenial condo
in this Disneyland
of globalization.

The Educational Impact of Auschwitz, 2004

This, my most recent effort at writing poetry, was "inspired" by a trip to Germany and Poland that I took with my friend and colleague, George Kliger. George invited me to accompany him as he revisited places associated with crucial events in his life before coming to Minnesota after 1945. He was born, raised and endured life in the ghetto at Lodz, Poland. George also survived Auschwitz.

The presiding Nazi
over the Auschwitz death camp
was a college president,
but without portfolio.
The camp offered experimental courses
in sadistic bodily torment
and the targeting of victims,
not for a criminal act,
but for ethnic identity.
The faculty at Auschwitz
first taught Mass Murder 101,
instantly copied and improved upon
by the world's nation-states.
Though the original text
may have been authored by Hitlerean
academics,
subsequent research and development
on the extermination
of your unwanted neighbors
has expanded beyond belief
from Himmler
to Saddam–Pol Pot.
As a daily routine, in 1942–44,
the Nazis used Cyclon B
to gas 2,000 noncombatant Jews
at a single shower party.
In 1945, ordinary Japanese people
by the 100,000s
were wiped out
in Tokyo, Nagasaki, and Hiroshima,
with a shower of American bombs,

both conventional and nuclear.
And two decades later,
from the American arsenal
of innovative military technology,
the plague of Agent Orange
was unleashed
in the jungles of Vietnam
to weaken the resolve
of guerilla resistance.
Echoes from the hallowed halls of
Auschwitz "U"
have been heard far and wide:
the Hutu slaughter of Tutsis
has earned the perpetrators
an "A" rating
in the field of committing genocide
with limited resources.
Serb violence against Bosnians,
like an earlier mass murder
of Serbs by Croatians,
has earned both victimizers
awards in the highly competitive field
of ethnic cleansing.
An Auschwitz trophy
in the "killing fields" competition
has been given for the murder of 1,000,000
Cambodians
by other Cambodians,
for the sake of an ideologue's dream.
Well-funded and popular
among the governing elites,
and having established
a new and promising program
on Islamic terrorism,
the legacy of Auschwitz "U"
looks brightly to an expanded enrollment
of peoples and cultures,
in the twenty-first century,
on the planet earth.

World History and the Philosophy of Life

ᘛᘚ

Henry Derozio; Influential Hindu College Teacher, 1962

In this third section, I shift from my poetic focus on travel of one sort or another, to what I broadly refer to as world history and the philosophy of life. Though my first poem is derived from my research on British Orientalism and the Bengal Renaissance, the tribute to this historical figure was not intended as scholarship. The persons I sought to write about in my poetry were not in politics, the bureaucracy, business or the military, but were among the more creative-minded intelligentsia.

A legend
already before
his corpse was cold,
this fiery Indo-Portuguese
stirred up
a Socratic rebellion
and died a Socratic death.
Nurtured by a renegade Scotsman
with a twisted back,
but a nimble mind,
young Derozio
imbibed the noble truths
of eighteenth-century France.
But he was
no mere political figure
with a flair
for propaganda.
Very early in life,
he was afflicted
with a passion for verse
to which he succumbed
with a Byronic posture.
Some British friends
were amused,
preferring instead
those who drank hard
and wrote epics
bemoaning their exile in India.
How could Derozio
not be an object
of ridicule?

A Byronic man-of-the-world
dying a virgin at twenty-three?
But Derozio's gift
to the modern
Indian nation
is no laughing matter.
Let them scoff
if they will,
but the first generation
of modern Bengal (1820s)
eager to change
their world,
were Derozio's students.
None came
from the missionary college
at Serampore,
nor the Sanskrit College
of the Brahmanical elite,
but from Hindu College
where the nineteen-year-old Derozio
began professing philosophy
and the literary arts.
Though he never
wrote a Bengali word,
he celebrated India
as a Greek island
of mythic splendor,
and freedom
a universal ideal,
not easily bartered for
in the marketplace
of nations.
Though his life
was tragically short,
and his lyrics
easily forgotten,
history has treated
this gifted pedagogue
with the sweet aroma
of immortality.

William Carey, Father of Modern Bengali Prose, 1964

This was a second effort at transforming what amounts to mountains of prose into a succinct statement of William Carey's contribution to Indian history.

Thanks to God, British Orientalism
and the Baptist Mission
at Serampore,
William Carey
intruded himself
into the history of India.
The cultural renaissance
of modern Hinduism
was born
in the lush jungles
and muddy soil
of Bengal.
It flowered
in Calcutta,
twin city
of British rule
and the Bengali mind.
And in the city,
a college for civil servants
was born;
William Carey,
Baptist missionary,
served on the faculty
from which
he gave to the Bengalis
a prose,
by raising the people's chatter
to the status
of a vernacular.
Carey wedded
the elegance of classical Sanskrit
to the contemporary demands
of the nineteenth-century world.

Carey's gift to India
came not from
Eurocentric Christian arrogance,
but Orientalist
intellectual curiosity
and assimilation.
We can only be thankful
that this expatriate missionary
born of the English peasantry,
began his herculean challenge
by reinventing a language
and literature,
that ultimately paved the way
for the Nobel laureate,
Rabindranath Tagore.

Sir William Jones and the Positive Side of British Colonialism, 1967

In this third tribute to a seminal figure of the Indian Renaissance, I also discuss some of the crucial ideas that I developed in my scholarship. This form of the poetic history of modern India is the result of amassing data, writing historical prose, then altering the expression to render it more compact and precise but without changing the meaning.

You were a brilliant humanist,
Sir William,
and belong properly
to the ages
of renaissance giants.
You were
among the legion of Orientalists
who plunged
into the unchartered ocean
of ancient India,
and emerged
with whole civilizations
clutched to their bosoms.
You were among the first,
Sir William,
and how noble
you were, sir.
While many
in the East India Company
spent their days
scheming bold plots
to rob
a helpless people,
like the Spaniards
in quest of gold,
you spent sleepless nights
learning languages
no longer spoken or read,
ascertaining
their kinship
and illuminating
their historic presence.

Are you not
India's Petrarch?
Perhaps more so,
since the world
you resurrected
was far more vast,
and the linguistic challenge
a hundred times greater.
Did you not
first espouse
the kinship between Europe and India,
sustained
at some remote time
by means of
an etymological chain,
stretched from the Gangetic plains
across Persia,
to pre-classical Greece and Rome?
In effect, sir,
you were Petrarch
to two glorious epochs:
your Asiatic Society of Bengal
spread the rediscovered
wisdom and art
of India's golden age
to the European
halls of learning;
and so, from the source
of British Orientalism,
the Emersons, Schopenhauers
and Hegels
intoxicated themselves
on this new exotic nectar,
opening
the ecumenical eye
to envision
the Eurasian past.

Orientalism, 1969

Orientalism is one of the most misunderstood historical concepts in our time. Its negative usage in the historiography of East-West relations can be traced to a legion of post-modern deconstructionists and the arch mythmaker, Edward Said. I recall when Said was invited to debate Orientalism at a conference dedicated to William Jones but he refused even to acknowledge our invitation.

Do we celebrate
or despair
when humans
usurp God's role
and create new paradigms
out of the void?
Even colonialism,
as evil
as it surely is,
has its heroes
who seek
virtue, knowledge and the arts.
There are those
who cross the frontiers
of history,
giving birth
to worlds long lost
to the collective consciousness.
Orientalists in India
were such
to be honored
as champions
of the reconstructed past.
From unintelligible script
on long-forgotten pillars
and rusty coins,
a Prinsep brother unraveled
Asokan India,
greater than today's
Indian nation-state;

whereas William Jones
broke a dozen trails
through the wilderness
of Indo-European tongues.
And the Colebrookes and Wilsons
established chronological guideposts,
to rescue civilization
from the black hole
of oblivion.
James Prinsep was another
of those gifted amateurs
sent to India
to mint coins.
But on his own,
Prinsep labored
long into the night
until he rediscovered
the Brahmi script.
And soon,
the historic Buddha
stood before him
offering salvation
to the suffering human race.
The Orientalist gift
of rediscovery
was of no small import:
Maurya and Gupta kings,
and poets,
like Kalidasa,
and temples
that fused the spirit
with iconographic splendor.
The Orientalist legacy:
a pre-Muslim golden age.

Angkor and Humanity's Fate Written on the Sands of Penang, 1971

Though Angkor represents Orientalism in the best sense of the term, my scholarly interest in the concept was not the intent of the poem. Cambodia's golden age of Angkor had been lost completely until the French period of colonial rule.

You and I, dear,
sit upon a platform of sand,
reading between the waves
sweet thoughts of recent days.
Even bitter memories
are now sweet thoughts
In the calm beauty
of a tropical night.

Do you recall the clash
between man and nature
at the ancient ruins
of Angkor?
Humankind here cleared space
to construct
a symphony in stone.
I know not
which is the greater beauty,
Angkor as it was:
a peopled universe
imbued with an inflated image
of its self-importance;
or Angkor today:
remains of a temple
rising like a sculptured mountain
above the encroaching green hell.
Voices depicting the commerce of life
or the eternal silence
of a civilization gone dead?

Here we are, my dear,
sifting through
the sands of Penang.
The archaeological ghost town of Angkor
haunts us still.
Is it the pulse
of resurrected time
that beats?
Is Angkor
like the lines
written in the sands of Penang
to be lost forever
in the rising tide?

Rammohun Roy: Father of Modern India, 1973

Though Rammohun Roy is an important historical figure in my first monograph on British Orientalism and the Bengal Renaissance, he is even more important in my second monograph on Brahmo Samaj and the Shaping of the Modern Indian Mind. This poem was written at the time of my second monograph and has been read several times to Unitarian congregations in the United States. Rammohun established a Unitarian Committee in Calcutta in 1823.

Even the Delhi crowd
hails this
Bengali Kulin Brahman
as Father
of the Modern Indian Nation.
We've had
many fathers of new nations:
Sun Yat-sen of China
or Mustafa Kemal of Turkey.
Rammohun was, however,
somewhat special
in that he was neither
lawyer nor general,
but an intellectual.

This Indian genius
preferred curiosity
to blind tradition,
and alienation for a cause,
to conformity
among his peers.
Rammohun searched
deep into the Hindu past
in quest
of a new identity.
From Islam,
he acquired
iconoclastic purity,
with a vision of God
that transcended
human fallibility.

The Upanishads taught him
diversity in the world of senses
was an illusion.

From Serampore Baptist Mission,
the stormy protests
of Luther and Calvin
reached Rammohun's ears;
he rejected the Trinity
as fraudulent idolatry
and sought the unadulterated Christ,
not in the intricacies
of canonical law,
but in the ethics of compassion.
Rammohun was no fool;
he met the Christian challenge
by finding Christ's message
in the ancient Hindu scriptures,
which were being reread
by the new type of Sanskritist
with the critical eye
of the rationalist.

And so the Brahmo Samaj was born
amid the defenders
of status quo Christianity
and Hinduism.
Hail to the rebirth
of modern India,
not by loss of soul
to the West,
nor by holding fast
to the decadent present,
but by reconstructing
the dynamic Indian past
and wedding it
to a hopeful future.

Durga Puja (Homage to the Goddess Durga), 1979

My historical interest at the time was the Hindu worship of woman as god as part of a larger interest in sexuality and religion in middle period Bengali history.

Sakti is the Hindu god
as woman
worshipped in her many aspects:
Lakshmi is wealth, Saraswati is music and art,
Kami is love, Kali is death
and Durga is the goddess as mother.

In Calcutta,
after the setting of a wintry sun,
beyond the muddy,
but hallowed waters of the Ganges,
thousands of city dwellers,
and those from the marshy villages,
crowd the streets
with festive delight
in praise of Durga.
Hindu female deities
are the true architects
of creation, harmony and destruction;
and we appeal to Sakti:
"defend us for another year
from the many faces of chaos".

But Durga is today
an altered image.
At one time,
she was a folk icon
close to the Indian soil;
she wore no fashionable sari.
But, today, she and her cohorts
reenact the eternal drama
according to the aesthetic
and sacred conception

of a Bombay movie studio.
Meanwhile, the Calcutta crowds
meander among the pandals
indulging their wants
with a Christmas spirit.
Days later,
the immersions begin,
and the goddess
is laid to rest
in the holy river.

Hinduism, 1979

Here I have tried to combine different concepts in the philosophy of the Hindu faith. It has certainly been one of my most difficult undertakings.

Some say Hinduism is a religion
left in the wake
of God's scorched earth policy;
others say,
it is existential thought
with its denial of history;
still others say,
it is merely
marigolds and melted butter.
Someone else has written:
"India is a jungle
where religion grows wild
and Brahmans
are the caretakers,
but not the gardeners."
Hinduism is also Tantra
at Konarak,
where the flesh and spirit
are lovingly joined
in one another's embrace.
I have also heard it said:
"if you scratch an Indian intellectual,
a Hindu saddhu will emerge."
One Indian mathematician
with a Soviet degree,
visits Benares regularly
to consult his astrologer.
I have been told
that God is the national drink of India,
and that his very presence
flows in the blood of a Hindu.
Hear the missionary proclaim:
"Hinduism is the faith

of an illiterate mass
oppressed by oppression itself."
Hear the Orientalist declare:
"the true Hinduism gave birth
to yoga and the Buddha,
to Kalidasa and Asoka,
and to a glowing age of gold."
But ages grow dark
from the incursions of Kali,
as the creative spirit
dies in a people.
In its place,
Hinduism was transformed
into a cluster of habitual acts,
among a people
now at the mercy
of a congenital epidemic
of weariness.

The Whole World Is a Jew, 1979

In a poem such as this, I was preparing myself for my growing interest in comparative world history, which I introduced as a course in the Department of History at the University of Minnesota just about this time.

Look straight between the eyes of the world
and you will find a Jew.
Ask an Indian exile in London
why Africans hated him so.
Why is a Chinese
a second-class Malaysian?
Do not the Parsis of Bombay
smell like Jews?
Why does one Marwari
help another Marwari
defraud a peasant?
Sukarno deported a thousand Chinese from Java
in a single week.
Huguenots were butchered
in the very heart
of Western Civilization.
Why has the colored face of a Japanese
grown a shade lighter
in the darkness of South Africa?
Does not the American black
wear his skin
like the nose of a Jew?
Look carefully
at your neighbor
or yourself,
and you will find a Jew.

A Father's Advice to the Newlyweds, 1989

Except for the last piece of advice, the poem is an embodiment of certain "eastern" ideas I thought appropriate in a verbal offering at my daughter's wedding reception. She had married Gavin Patterson, whom she had met in Scotland at the university.

Remember:
caste, class, race and gender
are Maya's masks;
we should all come together
in unity,
as do the rivers in the sea.
Remember:
never does hatred
cease by hatred;
hatred ceases by love.
Remember:
he who conquers an army
is a great general;
but she
who conquers herself
is the greatest of all victors.
Remember:
permanence is illusion
since the world is alive
with endless possibilities;
life is a rapid succession
of flickering images
as we cross
the short, painful distance
between birth and death.
Remember:
in the home,
follow the white path of peace;
but in the jungle
of human encirclement,
do unto others
before they do unto you.

A Day of Meditation and Peace at the Lake, 1983

Though I have meditated very often at Minnesota's magnificent lakes, I regret my failure to wed poetry to meditation.

White sail
on a drifting craft
vanishes
in the cloudy, fog-drenched lake
(like the blur of vaguely-defined issues).
Old, drab, gray-haired men
sit chit-chatting
at the pier,
casting lines
(the search for truth, as in the search for fish, often eludes us).
The thin-legged,
long-bodied jogger
huff-puffs
his circuitous circumnavigation
(endurance for life's pain requires training).
Others,
rather than jog,
prefer to promenade,
sense-sucking smells, sounds and sights
(only the quiet wanderer through life can observe its beauty).
The duck gropes for survival
within the four corners,
but other birds
soar above the blue water
or flip-flop
with fearless abandon
(man is Machiavelli; man is Michelangelo).

The Three Faces of Truth (December 31, 1999)

I do not know many people who would compose a poem of this sort on New Year's eve. I was never more convinced than on this occasion that poetry is some kind of inner voice demanding to be heard. When and why this happens we—in all probability—may never know.

I am no philosopher,
but I know
truth has three faces:
one has the cool, impassive look
of the scholar and scientist
in quest of
relevant or experimental data;
another betrays the comforting realism
of common sense,
or Robert Frost amid fenced-in neighbors
on a chilly New England morn;
and the third face
is most of us earthlings,
with indescribable fears,
world-weary prejudices
and deep caverns of hate.
One truth reaches out
for the essence of matter;
another yearns for a neighborly ethic;
the third truth arises
from a confrontation with nature,
both physical and human.
The first truth
has uncovered civilizations,
split the atom,
and hurled the human race into space;
the second has engendered
commerce, politics and the family;
the third truth
contains the fate of the masses
to a world
of hell on earth.

Are there not truths
beyond the indulgence
of scientistic self-importance,
common-sense complacency,
and a chronic sense of the life-threatening?
Are we not captives of illusion
wherever we stand?
Why are we born,
when we live all too briefly,
then die forever?

An Obscure Obituary Notice: Our Century as a Burial Ground, 1999

This poem was not merely written on New Year's eve but on the eve of the new millennium. I wonder if most historians of ideas were as much influenced by emotion as I was in their evaluation of twentieth-century thought.

Is not our century
the burial ground
for nineteenth-century ideas?
The rock of Gibraltar
may stand
but the isms
of Disraeli and Churchill
have passed into history.
European socialists
signed their death warrant
when, in 1914,
they chose war
above the welfare
of the human race.
Why have liberal values
turned flabby
with prosperity,
and become the badge
of creature comfort?
The market place
of laissez faire,
and its cousin,
the democratic state,
lie buried in the ruins
of corporate greed.
Ought we not plant
a flower of reverence
in honor of
nineteenth-century genius,
which lies in the graveyard
of the idea
as wishful thinking?

Rebelling
against god and morality
as parental misfits,
Nietzsche embraced the superman.
The Comtes and Spencers
who saw nothing but glory
in our future,
may have
idled their time away
in dreams
that pictured reality
through rose-colored filters.
There lies Victorian thought
which died gracefully
with English self-restraint.
It is often said
that creative thought, itself,
lies buried—
without mourners—
on a hillside
near the graveyard.
Have not foundations
seduced intellectuals
by diverting their quest
for ideologies of salvation?
A foundation fellow
named Marx or Darwin or Hegel
would have been sitting
in the draughty reading room
of the British Library,
gathering knowledge
from dusty volumes
to enhance
one's scholarly status.

Sharing with Walter the Wisdom of the Upanishads, 2002

I do not know why I feel it necessary to offer "oriental" philosophic advice to my children during their betrothal or marriage. This poem based on my reading of the Upanishads, compiled by Indian thinkers sometime between the ninth and sixth centuries B.C., *was the source for my advice to my son, Walter, on his wedding to Judy.*

Before Buddha, Confucius, Zarathustra and Christ,
India gave to the world
the poetic dialogues
of the Upanishads,
a corpus of wisdom
both authorless and godless.
Truth lay
in the liberation of self
from an ego-centered life:
the blind foolishly prize
the externalities
of wealth, power and conceit;
they wallow
in phenomenal multiplicity;
the blind are misled
into the duality
of race, gender and class.

The clear-sighted are inward-looking
and achieve wisdom from within.
Above all superficial knowledge
is atma, the true mind
of the liberated soul,
hailing wisdom
as rooted
in the oneness of all existence.
Look deeply for the light within,
to root out
the illusion of diversity.
There are no races,
only the human race.
There is no nation,
only the world exists.

Reaction to Those Dying Around Me, 2005

This poem is a reaction to death and dying around me. I might also mention that I turned seventy-five years of age in 2005.

Death is a perennial traveler
from hell,
a democratic force
that equalizes
the social distance
between rich and poor.

Death is the true force
of nature,
offering those
born of flesh
the illusion of permanence.

Progress and perfectability
glamorize
the aura of the life force,
but the cyclical pattern
of human experience
is in death's dominion.

Religion may appear other-worldly,
but it is a game,
invented and played
by life advocates,
to achieve life everlasting;
and all we know
of the transit
is the decomposition
of our bodily parts.

Whether soul
is the true home
of human salvation,
or another pile of rhetoric
in the warehouse
of human wishful thinking,
it is only
for death to declare.

Creation of the life force
may be heard
in the sudden emergence
of sounds
in symphonic unison.
But death concludes
the music of life
by muffling our cries
for survival,
and returning us
to the universe of silence.

Looking Ahead to an Afternoon in the Global Year, 2050 A.D.

This is the only poem I ever wrote in which I predict the future. It has been difficult enough for me to make sense of the past. From another angle of vision, one could argue that predicting the future is really a comment on the good and bad one perceives in one's own time.

A factory
in the distance
belches black dust
from its phallus-like protrusion.
The daily sky
is without sunrise
or sunset,
while noon
is blanketed
in polluted darkness.
The once
pleasantly-alluring green earth
is now
but a dream
of yesteryear.
At mid-century,
the color green
has ceased to exist.
Where now
are the lush pastures and forests?
The summer leaves
are but a memory
of a bygone age;
and the autumn leaves,
as well,
now colorless,
drift helplessly
in the sterile winds
of "progress."

The Romantic Lover and His Conversion to the Church of Eros

Isolation and the Pangs of Remorse, 1948

This poem begins the final section on the many manifestations of love which is treated, as were other sections, chronologically. In the first poem, we are transported back to the University of Miami where I bemoan separation from Lorraine, who was my girlfriend in the Platonic sense.

Alone and friendless,
I am seated
a momentary distance
from the campus club.
For hours,
a deafening silence;
then suddenly,
an explosion
of shouts and laughter
by students
in a mood of jovial restlessness.
Soon the air is ablaze
with big band sounds of swing:
Stan Kenton's *How High the Moon*
drifts ever upwards
from the club,
pausing only in the sky
to settle
on a glimmer of daylight.
Then my sight
shifts inward
and I see Lorraine
with my mind's eye.
And soon,
I suffer once more
the pain of separation
and love lost,
in the dark labyrinth
of unfamiliar distance
between Miami and New York.

First Poem of Loving Encounters with Susan, 1948

Susan changed my life in love entirely. I intended the poem to convey that it was not simply a loss of virginity on my part but that the event has to be understood in the context of a multidimensional relationship.

Our first encounter
in geology class,
between a scientific illiterate
and a naturephiliac.
Second encounter
at a Chopin concert
in Miami Senior High,
between an adolescent, romantic dilettante
and a gifted, but thwarted pianist.
Third encounter
in world literature class,
between a pigmy amid the classics
and a bookish prima donna.
Fourth encounter
in an ornithology field trip,
between an uninitiated bird-watcher
and a bird-watching devotee.
Fifth encounter
on a bed of sand
during a moonless night
on a silent beach,
between a male virgin
until that fateful historic moment,
and a vulnerable female
deliciously in heat.

Confessions of an Eighteen-Year-Old Romantic, 1948

I included this poem in the section to show that however physical in a normal sense our relationship was, it never altered my romantic attitude to Susan and to other women I loved.

The morning,
nothing but gray mist
settling over foggy trails
in the forest
where I hiked.
A succession
of sunless days
covered the woody terrain
with a perennial gloom.
But then you appeared,
dear Susan,
and the world was bright once more.
You, loving creature,
are my woman
partaking in godliness
and giving meaning
to existence.
How sweet are the hours
as we melt
into one another's arms,
crazed by
unlimited, uninhibited joy.
How fortunate
to have been pierced
by Cupid's arrow
at the order of a goddess.

Memories of Love and Marriage, 1974

I am deeply thankful for experiencing precisely what this poem is about. Considering the fragility of life, I look upon myself as having been most fortunate for being granted these wonderful years.

How the fates conspired
that summer in Maine
to arrange
our coming together:
two summer counselors
on a Sunday break;
the fatal attraction
between arts and crafts
and outdoor adventure,
between the creative soul
and the traveler
along the trails
of natural beauty.

Then Philadelphia,
where I courted my beloved
in an Ivy League
off-campus flat.
Again,
the undeniable magnetism
between a humanities major
and a student
of occupational therapy.

There followed
the parental encounters
in New Jersey
and Wisconsin,
between an East European,
Yiddish heritage
and deep-rooted
anglo-ethnicity:

a daughter
of the American Revolution
and a father
born in Gravesend
on the English Channel.

I admired you so
for converting
to the orthodox faith
of my ma-pa,
so that you could marry
an alienated
Jewish intellectual
from Paterson,
city of William Carlos Williams
and Allen Ginsberg.
We were also
elegantly wed
in your Wisconsin home.

It all began
in a blissful marital abode
across from Grant's Tomb
on Riverside,
along the Hudson
in upper Manhattan.
Our daily paths
took me to NYU
in Greenwich Village,
where I pursued
a Master of the Arts
in the study
of the Renaissance;
whereas you studied
the Fine Arts
at Queen's College,
and taught the same
to gifted adolescents
at Music and Art High School.

Soon our adventurous spirit
drove us to Chicago:
you taught
at John Dewey's
paradigmatic Lab School;
and I, a total stranger
to the Asian world,
chose the exotic field
of Indian studies,
in the time dimension,
at the University of Chicago,
where I began
my circuitous path to the doctorate.

How glorious those memories:
intellectual growth
and thousands of reciprocal,
ravishing intimacies;
and the day
we celebrated
the Ford Foundation grant to India,
which three years later,
became a dissertation on
British Orientalism and the Bengal Renaissance;
then years after that,
became a prize-winning monograph
at the annual gathering
of the American Historical Association.
You and I shared
every moment of it,
living intensely,
both in sickness and in health.

A colleague once said:
"Storks don't bring babies;
doctoral dissertations do that."
And so it happened
that our daughter was born
when I professed
the history of India
at the University of Missouri.
Could it be
that tenure at the
University of Minnesota
brought forth our son?
And there you were,
on the eve of birth,
insisting
upon typing my manuscript
on comparative Asian civilizations.
The Axial Age in Eurasia
was born
between labor pains
as a first draft.

Though subsequent years
have not treated us kindly,
I am thankful
that remembrances of things
long past,
are not lost
necessarily,
but remain a gift
from one loving heart
to another.

From Bangladesh to Bennington (Paradise Regained), 1975

In 1975, I was invited to be a fellow at the think tank in Bangladeshi Studies at Rajshahi University in Rajshahi, Bangladesh. I worked with an excellent teacher, a medical anthropologist from Bennington College, Vermont. Truly amazing, as I look back now, is that the two of us studied the erotic mysticism of medieval Bengal in an Islamic country.

No tormented soul
in this resort,
nor poverty of spirit.
Though March winds
blow icy rain
and the dreary mist
spreads its blanket
of gloom,
my love and I
bathe in our own
reflected sunlight
around the pure splendor
of our love.
Leafless trees
and the barren yellow fields
of winter,
are radiantly green
in the midday sun.
Utopia here,
with restful, timeless space;
bird calls and sensuality;
the transcendence
of warped and senseless existence
as two mystics embrace,
their bodies sacredly interlocked
in a supreme gesture
of holy rapture.
It is written
in the Bible
of the Left-Handed mystics:
the bedroom is

the true church of the Supreme Goddess
and the true faith
lies between the sheets;
love and tenderness
are her scripture,
and divine unity
is achieved
by the interpenetration
of devotees.

The Church of Eros, 1975

While we indulged ourselves in this Hindu tradition, the political situation in Bangladesh was hardly stable. Mujibur Rahman, who had led the freedom movement against Pakistan in 1971, was assassinated just prior to our arrival in the country in June of 1975. The coup had also disposed of his ministers, who were in prison.

Dearest,
fear not
being consumed
by love;
it is death
we may fear,
or hate,
but not the sweetness
of a loving heart.
Death waits
in the closet of despair,
for the separation
of lovers,
hoping to dismantle
the joyous present
and the innocent bliss
of true love.
Take heart
in the mansion of eros,
which is
the true church
of life everlasting.

A Promenade with My Love in a Bangladeshi Jungle, 1975

In this stroll through a tropical jungle, the poet goes beyond erotic mysticism to a sacred sensitivity about all that lives in the natural world. Living in proximity to a jungle in 1975 was totally different in many ways to living in the urban environment of Calcutta on earlier research assignments.

We stood on the threshold
of this life-infested world
as worshippers
of sacred love,
seeking to understand
why humans, alone,
consumed their flesh
in the fires
of a loving embrace.
All mount
the mare of pleasure,
seeking the prey
of ecstatic delight.
Only we
endow the merry chase
with holy meaning.

Each female creature
is afire
with every stroke and kiss,
but in your eyes
I see also
mirrored
the spiritual passion
of the Lord Krishna.
Those who
spiritualize sex
can transform
the rocky void
into a lush jungle
of pungent
and exotic fruit.

My love has now
become sensitive
to the death
of a single leaf;
she can now muffle the deafening roar
of an insect
trampling a blade of grass;
her ears strain
to capture
each delicate murmur of life;
her eyes search out
the hidden aesthetic
underlying
the mysterious forces
of nature.

Muslim Woman, 1975

(Dedicated to Noor-e-Hafza)

I should point out that there were also "liberated" Bangladeshi women who were on the faculty of Rajshahi University and in no way resemble the profile of a Muslim woman that the poem suggests. Nevertheless, I do believe the poem has validity in depicting a type of Islamic woman who still very much exists.

The veil of fear
still conceals
your true self;
purdah, invisible,
but hard as steel,
still imprisons
your impulses.
And you submit
to habit and tradition
rather than
existential choice.
Where does feminine beauty lie?
In your alluring
black kajol eyes?
In the child-like
innocent simplicity
of your face?
Or in the hidden
subtlety of your thoughts?
Can any woman
achieve full equality
with a man?
Is your slavery
the biological handiwork
of a malevolent God
who fashioned
the gendered human condition
out of malice?
Or are your chains
man-made contrivances?

What is freedom
but the realization
of a dream?
And what is the dream?
That life
runs its own course
unencumbered by philosophy,
uncorroded by theology;
petty minds
imbued with narrow vision.
Are we imprisoned
by our fate,
or is life a struggle
to achieve the impossible?
Are you imprisoned, dear lady,
in a tower
of social decadence?
Oh, Muslim woman!
Is learning
only an ornament
to be worn
like a glittering necklace?
Or is it a lamp
in the darkness of your self,
to win
human self-respect
and a ladder to a reality
beyond slavery?

Reverence for the Divine Woman as a Multi-Faceted Goddess, 1979

In 1979, I was very much into the worship of woman as God in Hinduism. In the previous section, I included a poem on my reaction to the way Durga, the goddess as mother, was worshipped during her holiday in Calcutta in December of 1979. In this poem, I cover the varied aspects of the goddess, concluding with her loving nature comparable with Aphrodite and Venus.

It was a Bengali friend
who first introduced me
to the worship
of Sakti,
or the spiritual essence
of woman
as the true divine source
behind the wheel
of birth and rebirth.
You are the creative power
of art and learning,
or Saraswati,
without which
beauty and intellect
would be an empty dream.
You are energetic endeavor
and successful enterprise,
or Lakshmi,
without which
inertia would rule
a changeless universe.
You are mother
to all earthly existence,
or Durga,
without whom
the world would be a cross
between an endless desert
and a perennial world
of winter.
You are the destroyer

of life
and the keeper
of death's dominion,
or Kali,
without whom
there would be
a life everlasting
of pain and suffering.

You are, above all,
the goddess of the bedchamber,
keeper of sanctified
sensual pleasure,
or Kami
without whom
there would be no
warmth and tenderness,
or moments of joyful love
snatched from the jaws
of a loveless existence.

Transformations, 1985

Dulali is a fictitious name for a Bengali woman I came to know after I parted from the Bennington anthropologist. The poem does not do justice to her warmth and generosity as a human being.

First Dulali:
you stood there,
a Bengali female pope,
together
with Sakti at your side,
pontificating your discourse
in the manner
of a sacred text.

Second Dulali:
we held hands
and my lonely heart
began to stir
as Bengali songs
filled the room
and male voices,
unwittingly,
provided the prelude
to a new love.

Third Dulali:
I embraced
my image of delight
in the dark room;
it seemed
as if both of us
were the chosen
of Kama's kingdom.
But the real object
of my love
remained distant and ambivalent.
Forgive me

for preferring
dusty archives
to your heated embrace.

Fourth Dulali:
you are a
phantom image
of what
might have been
but never was.
In the winter
of my despair,
it is far worse
to feel remorse
for a love
that could have been,
to a love lost.

My Love and the Loveless Object of My Love, 2000

This is one of the few poems I ever wrote on being rejected by someone I wanted very much to cultivate as a loving friend. Fortunately, such periods of despair have been infrequent.

Whether from Minneapolis
to anywhere on earth,
any travel is miniscule
as against
the interplanetary
psychic distance
that separates us.
If only as
I could surmount
your frigid world
of indifference
and strike up
a single spark of love.
But all has been in vain
since the object
of my devotion
has anchored herself
on a sterile star
surrounded by an astromoat
that entraps such as I,
within whom,
flow the divine juices
of the erotic Lord Kama.
No weapon
in the army of Eros
can penetrate your shield
of frigid transcendence.
If only
I could deconstruct
the dragon
of your denial
to win your love.
I had once

a resplendent vision
of you and I
treading the same path,
arm in arm,
through the lush garden
of our love together.
But the flowers of my hope
have been crushed
and lie lifeless
in the barren field.
My despair
has become
a mountain of grief
as I bemoan
the cruel design
of my fate.

To My New Friend, 2000

This was the first poem in appreciation of a new and loving friendship.

A global fountain
of charitable intentions;
queen of the inconsistent back stroke;
a tall blade of grass
reaching for the moon
at sunset;
a proud hiker
boldly walking the trails of life.
Forgive the intruder
who enters your pathway,
for we are soul mated,
you and I,
reborn to share once more
some unknowable fate.

Love and Virginity, 2001

These lines came to me one afternoon while seated in an outdoor café reflecting on how a relationship had changed from friendship to love.

Falling in love
restores my virginity.
No matter how often it happens,
the thirst
for the fresh water
of the spring,
is always—
a virginal thirst.

Attributes of My Beloved, 2003

Interestingly, for me, the same qualities in my beloved which endear me to her as a person also endear me to her as a lover.

Her Catholicism
is a religion of Humanity:
not a sectarian faith
remembered for the Inquisition
and the burning of witches;
not Christological metaphysics
but faith in earthly progress;
not the brutality
of crusading armies
waving their ideological flags.
Capturing
a corner of darkness,
she prays in silence
for liberation
from tribal strife
and the energizing
discourse of peace
for the triumph of one world.

My Chinese Woman of the World, 2004

I first met my Chinese woman friend while researching my developing interest in comparative genocide which became a book I co-authored with Eric Markusen entitled Total War and Genocide in the Twentieth Century. *I am proud of her perseverance as a survivor and her ability to retain her humor and humanity throughout her ordeal.*

Born into a Chinese Hainan
family
which had crossed
land and sea
to what was then
Cambodge,
where they settled
among Cambodians
as the Jews of
Southeast Asia.
Brought up
among fisherfolk,
and schooled
in the mode
of the mother country,
she flowered
into sinicized womanhood
with a keen ear for
neighboring spoken tongues
and a sensitive eye
for the fine art
of painting.
To no one's surprise,
she mated
and delivered
three offspring.
But history and fate
were less predictable
as former
French Indo-China
erupted into
a killing field;

and my woman
fled the murderous wrath
of Nixon and Pol Pot
as a refugee.
Then as a refugee,
once more,
the family
escaped Vietnam
as boat people
sailing the South China Seas,
eluding pirates
all the way
to a Thai camp.
As a displaced
global wanderer
of the twentieth century,
she went from Hong Kong
to the Philippines,
to the Dakotas,
to Minnesota.
She was reborn
in Minneapolis
with English as
a step-mother tongue,
and the mechanical arts
qualifying her
as a cog
in an assembly line.

With my mother
in her final years
drifting into oblivion,
my Chinese woman
was a bastion
of formidable patience
and a blanket
of comforting warmth.
As for me,

my Chinese woman
has been
a manipulative,
passionate romantic,
determined
to retain our bond
of intimacy
throughout the here
and the hereafter.

Ode to the Blue and White Football Jersey, 2004

I conclude my volume of poetry with a light-hearted poem on the history of my football jersey, which today serves a totally different purpose from its original function.

Oh, well-knitted fabric
of high school days
that housed a bulk
of a slow-witted footballer;
you preferred
body-clashing
and painfully rolling
in the gravel
to homework
on a Saturday afternoon.

The jersey
has travelled to many countries
since then;
it no longer houses
the jock-bulk
of yesteryear
collecting dirt and dust
on a field of battle.
The jersey
became a multi-purpose
wrap-a-round
for a wandering academic
when crossing climes
in need of warmth,
or as a shield
against wind and sun.

Today,
the jersey
resides in
the closet of my despair;
it is a shrine